Title: "The People Are the Prize, Not the Profit: Building Empathetic Teams for High Performance"

Author: Kristina Villarini

Year of Publication: 2024

Copyright © 2024 Kristina Villarini

All rights reserved.

No part of this book may be reproduced, distributed, or transmitted in any form or by any means, including photocopying, recording, or other electronic or mechanical methods, without the prior written permission of the author, except in the case of brief quotations embodied in critical reviews and certain other noncommercial uses permitted by copyright law.

For permission requests, please contact: support@theempatheticleader.com.

Disclaimer: The information in this book is provided for informational purposes only and is not intended as a substitute for medical, legal or financial professional advice.

The People Are the Prize, Not the Profit:

Building Empathetic Teams for High Performance

To my incredible wife, Arielle: your belief in me keeps me going, and your smile and laughter keeps me sane.

To my loving, chaotic, and beautiful family, who have stood by me through every twist and turn of my journey. I see you, and I love you.

To every person who has supported me, from near and far—you know who you are—thank you for encouraging me, even when I fall short.

Every single one of you make The Empathetic Leader possible.
Every day. Thank you for your patience, your passion, and your unwavering support.

This book is for all of you, for every leader out there who's ever felt lost, overwhelmed, or just plain human...

This one is for US.

Here's to the power of empathy and to growing, together.

Table of Contents (TOC)

- **A Note from the Author**
- **Introduction**
- **Chapter 1: The Power of Empathetic Hiring**
    - Understanding Empathetic Hiring
    - Examples of Empathetic Behaviors to Look For
    - Conducting Empathy-Focused Interviews
    - Examples of Successful Empathetic Frameworks in Modern Day Companies
    - The Human Potential of People
    - Looking Ahead
- **Chapter 2: Thoughtful SOPs for a Thriving Team**
    - What Are Standard Operating Procedures (SOPs)?
    - The Importance of SOPs in an Organization
    - Implementing SOPs Effectively
    - Methods for Regularly Reviewing and Updating SOPs
- **Chapter 3: Retaining an Empathetic Team**
    - The Role of Empathy in Team Retention
    - The Cost of High Turnover and the Benefits of Retention
    - Building a Supportive Work Environment
    - Strategies for Empathetic Leadership
    - Handling Conflict with Empathy
- **Chapter 4: Positive Relationships**
    - The Impact of Positive Relationships on Performance
    - Building Trust and Rapport
    - Maintaining Positive Relationships Over Time
- **Chapter 5: Achieving High Performance through Empathy**
    - The Link Between Empathy and Performance
    - How Empathy Drives Performance
    - Measuring Success with Empathy
- **Examining Empathetic Teams**
- **Conclusion**
    - Chapter Recap

- o The Future of Leadership is Empathetic
- **Final Thoughts**
    - o Embrace the Journey
    - o Motivated Empowerment
    - o The People Are the Prize
- **Index**
- **References**

A Note from the Author:

Thank you for deciding to invest in people.

While this book is a collection of some of the important things I have learned throughout my career, it's also a celebration of the people who made my success possible. It's a rebuke of those who continue to manage "one way" or "their way":
They are the hammer, and the people are the nails.

Across two decades of my career, I've seen hard managers, bad managers, no managers, and mismanagement. In each of those identities is a collection of failures, and a manager who likely failed them while they were on their journey to management.
And the cycle continues… Until we break it.

We are at a critical juncture in the labor market: people are taking less money simply to NOT BECOME a manager. They are also willing to wait until the right fit comes along. These individuals do not see joy in management, and they don't want to work for clowns. Mostly, they want zero responsibility for the outputs of others.

We have lost the plot. Management of others is a gift, because the people are the prize.

If this is the first time you have been introduced to the idea of empathetic leadership aka managing people with purpose, welcome to our community.

Have an open mind, and no matter where you are in your leadership journey, whether as a seasoned pro, a new manager, or even someone who is trying to shape the culture with no direct reports.

Now, before we dive in, I must share a quick **warning**.

This book may cause sudden outbursts of empathy, uncontrollable nodding, and a strong urge to revolutionize your workplace culture.

Side effects may include seeing the best in people, hiring for character traits as well as talent, building stronger teams, and, in extreme cases, having your employees enjoy coming to work.

Further still, they may actually like *you* and working *for you*.

If you experience any of these symptoms, congratulations—
you're becoming an empathetic leader.

Proceed with compassion.

Introduction

The pressures of leadership and management have reached unprecedented levels and expectations. We're juggling global crises, personal challenges, and workplace dynamics that can feel overwhelming. Meanwhile, we are supposed to also be good parents, role models, neighbors, spouses, and citizens.

We are supposed to be *LEADERS*.

So, you're not alone if you find yourself wondering how to navigate the daily demands of, at the very least, your professional life.

How do you maximize the "ROI" of leadership (and power), while striving to create a positive and productive environment for your team?

At the heart of effective leadership lies a simple yet powerful truth:
The people are the prize, not the profit.

I said this aloud in a room full of entrepreneurs in Nashville while noodling over the idea of this (and several other) books.

But the reaction was palpable and significant enough that this book became a critical corner piece of the puzzle that is management and leadership.

So, here we are.

Within these pages is the knowledge I've gained in the process of interviewing and hiring thousands of people, and the greatest privilege of my life: building and managing teams.

My lessons are your learnings, and those learnings are opportunities.
But your application can and should be different, because your teams and experiences are.
This is NOT intended to be a replacement for your experiences, instincts or knowledge of your people. But for the love of all that is holy, please

use this if you have no idea how to hire, empower, and retain teams that win.

We don't talk about the secret sauce of high performance enough: When you prioritize the well-being, growth, and satisfaction of your team, profits and performance naturally follow.

The Importance of Empathy in Leadership

Empathy got a bad rap. It was considered a "soft" skill for so long that we abandoned it all together. But the strong, modern leader has figured out that it is an essential trait, not a nice-to-have. And while many old-fashioned leaders still unfortunately consider it to be a "soft" skill, we have seen what has happened to leaders who kept drinking their own juice for too long. Their time will come.

The ability to understand and share the feelings of others is no longer just a nice-to-have—it's a must-have. In a world where work-life boundaries are increasingly blurred and stress levels are off the damn charts, empathetic leadership can make all the difference.

Empathy helps leaders to connect with their teams on a deeper level, building a sense of trust and respect. It enables you to see things from your team's perspective, anticipate their needs, and respond to their concerns with genuine care and compassion.

This not only improves individual well-being, but also transforms workplace dynamics, creating an environment where the little things take care of themselves. If a person feels trusted and supported every day to do their job, something strange could happen… They may just do their jobs.

When individuals are doing their jobs at a high level and a culture of support and teamwork is encouraged, collaboration and innovation can thrive.

Empathy as a foundation of your management and culture IS the winning strategy.

When you can identify and correctly deploy empathy, you see people for who they are, and not simply as outputs. You can understand their motivations, their struggles, their hopes, and fears. But it's not one size fits all.

You're going to have to listen to and learn from all of your colleagues and team members to maximize their performance.

How Empathy Transforms Workplace Dynamics

By shifting the focus from tasks and outcomes to people and relationships, the air in the rooms you're in changes. When employees feel understood and valued, they are more engaged, motivated, and willing to contribute their best efforts. They're also willing to help each other.

When you get this right, people have higher job satisfaction, there's lower churn, and you'll see better overall performance.

An empathetic workplace is one where open communication is encouraged, feedback is constructive, and conflicts are resolved with understanding and respect. It's a place where diverse perspectives are welcomed, and every team member feels a sense of belonging.

This positive atmosphere not only boosts morale but also drives the team towards achieving common goals with purpose. They're not working as individuals to hit goals, they're working within a team, for the company to succeed.

Here is what we're going to explore together:

- Empathetic Hiring: How to identify and attract candidates who not only have the right skills, but also the EQ to contribute to your team.

- Thoughtful SOPs: How to design and implement Standard Operating Procedures that support and enhance your team's work, rather than stifling their creativity and autonomy.
- Retention: We'll dive into techniques for building a supportive and engaging work environment that encourages loyalty and reduces turnover.
- Positive Relationships: Understand the power of positive relationships in driving team performance and achieving your big picture goals.

Nowhere in here did I mention anything about "workplace as family" or having a pool table in your office, or any of the nonsense marketing BS that has emerged to trick people into believing they matter at work. These places are eventually exposed as the biggest meat grinders in the world.

The only way to treat people in the workforce as if they matter is to believe it and then codify it in your DNA, culture and values.

I'm happy to be your spirit guide as you learn exactly how and why you should be leading with empathy and recognizing that your teams are more than just employees—they are individuals with unique strengths, aspirations, and potential.

By putting people *first*, you'll not only create a more harmonious and motivated workplace, but also drive sustainable and long-term success.

Chapter 1: The Power of Empathetic Hiring

By now, you should be at least *a little* curious about whether empathy can make a difference between building robust, resilient, and high-performing teams and teams that are pretty much the opposite.

Empathetic hiring transcends traditional recruitment practices by prioritizing emotional intelligence along with skills and qualifications. It acknowledges that the true strength of a company lies not just in its brand, products or services, but in its people.

So, what is it we are looking for?

Understanding Empathetic Hiring

When we are recruiting individuals, we want to attract those who possess the ability to understand and share the feelings of others. This approach focuses on ensuring that new hires can connect with colleagues, foster a supportive environment, and contribute to a positive culture. This should include discussions with candidates about their prior teams, how they interact with others, how they resolve conflict, and what their management style is like.

Many top performing individuals, especially from Sales backgrounds, struggle to shift from the "put as many points on the board as possible" mentality to the "team-first/people-first" mentality I am advocating for. This is not to say that you should not hire those individuals! However, in my experience, these individuals do require some time to adjust to the culture we are trying to build for long-term success.

I have found that empathetic managers create more empathetic employees, so coaching is a must. Empathetic employees communicate more effectively, resolve conflicts well, and support one another. That is what we want! If we can hire employees that have some of these traits already established, they can act as culture carriers.

When employees see each other as people, it frees up your brain power and time to manage the things that require your skill set and does not require you to referee shouting matches and other pettiness.

When all these dominoes fall, they lead to stronger teams and better production.

As employees feel more understood and valued, they are more likely to stay with the company, reducing turnover and associated costs. This is interesting to keep in mind as you are talking to candidates. If someone has left a company after a short time, it does not always mean that they have no loyalty or career aspirations. They may have been in a toxic culture, or one that did not prioritize people.

Ask if they would like to stay at your company for a long time and see how they answer. Many people have never even been invited to, either by opportunity or by career advancement!

People that are more invested in their teams will work well together and try harder to understand each other's perspectives. They are more likely to share ideas and develop creative solutions. Most importantly, empathetic teams connect better with clients, understanding their needs and building stronger, more trusting relationships.

As you are trying to find candidates who demonstrate empathy, you should use a deliberate approach during the interview process. It's not just about asking the right questions, but about observing behaviors and responses that indicate a candidate's ability to empathize.

Let's walk through some questions:

- Behavioral Questions: Ask candidates to describe past experiences that required empathy. This helps assess their ability to relate to others and handle interpersonal situations.
    - Example: "Can you tell me about a time when you had to put yourself in

someone else's shoes to solve a problem?"
- Scenario-Based Questions: Present hypothetical situations to see how candidates would respond, emphasizing their thought process and emotional intelligence.
    - Example: "How would you handle a situation where a team member is consistently underperforming due to personal issues?"
- Active Listening: Pay attention to how candidates respond to your questions. Do they listen attentively, ask follow-up questions, and show genuine interest in the conversation?

Examples of Empathetic Behaviors to Look For

- Active Listening: Candidates who listen carefully and respond thoughtfully demonstrate a key component of empathy.

- Non-Verbal Cues: Look for open body language, such as nodding, maintaining eye contact, and mirroring. Be cautious of candidate's who *only* mirror your behavior, and don't express themselves freely.
- Emotional Awareness: Candidates who can articulate their own emotions and show sensitivity to the feelings of others are likely to possess high emotional intelligence.

Conducting Empathy-Focused Interviews

Conducting interviews with empathy in mind requires a shift from traditional methods.

Here's a step-by-step guide to help you through the process:

- Set the Tone: Begin with a friendly and open demeanor. Let candidates know that honesty and authenticity are valued.

- o Create a Comfortable Environment: Ensure the interview setting is relaxed and inviting. This helps candidates feel at ease and be themselves.
- Use Open-Ended Questions: Ask questions that encourage candidates to share more about their experiences and thought processes.
  - o Sample Question: "Describe a situation where you had to support a team member who was struggling."
- Incorporate Scenarios: Present realistic scenarios relevant to the role.
  - o Sample Scenario: "Imagine you're leading a project and one of your team members is dealing with a personal crisis. How would you manage this situation?"
- Reflective Listening: Show that you're listening by reflecting back what the candidate says. This not only makes them feel heard but also helps you understand their perspective better.

Examples of Successful Empathetic Frameworks in Modern Day Companies

Salesforce: Salesforce has a strong commitment to creating an inclusive and empathetic workplace. The company focuses on employee well-being, diversity, and giving back to the community.
- **Empathetic Hiring:** Salesforce actively seeks to build a diverse workforce by implementing policies that ensure equal opportunities for all candidates.
- **Empathetic Framework:** Salesforce's Ohana culture emphasizes family, trust, customer success, and innovation, fostering a supportive environment.

Buffer: Buffer is known for its transparent and empathetic company culture, prioritizing the well-being and development of its employees.
- **Empathetic Hiring:** Buffer's hiring process includes values-based questions and a focus on candidates who align with the company's

core values of transparency, positivity, and self-improvement.
- **Empathetic Framework:** Buffer offers extensive mental health support, flexible work arrangements, and encourages open communication about challenges employees face.

The Human Potential of People

Empathetic hiring is not just about filling positions; it's about recognizing and nurturing the human potential within everyone. When you prioritize empathy, you create an environment where employees feel seen, heard, and valued. This leads to a more engaged workforce that is motivated to contribute their best work.

One quick shift you can make today to slowly shift away from the old-fashioned models:

Lead beyond titles! Leadership should not be expected only from those with formal titles. Every employee has the potential to lead by modeling empathetic behavior and creating a culture of understanding and support. Encourage your team members to take initiative, show compassion, and create the work environment they want. When everyone in your organization embraces empathy, it transforms the entire workplace.

Looking Ahead

Empathetic hiring sets the stage for a more cohesive, innovative, and resilient team. It will also allow you to set your company apart in the marketplace by being a place that values people.

As we move forward in this book, we will explore how to maintain this empathetic approach throughout the employee lifecycle, from onboarding to development and retention. By embedding empathy into every aspect of your company, you will build a workplace where people are truly the prize, and success follows naturally.

In the upcoming chapters, we will delve deeper into designing thoughtful SOPs, retaining teams, and leveraging relationships to achieve high performance.

Chapter 2: Thoughtful SOPs for Thriving Teams

To create a high-performing, empathetic workplace you must start with the right foundation, as a building is only as good as the structure it is built on.

If you don't currently have Standard Operating Procedures (SOPs), hopefully this chapter will help you reconsider.

It is worth saying that I assumed some things about the form and function of your workplace to write this book: that you currently have a team, that you're trying to figure out how to lead a team, you want to lead a team well or improve how you're doing now, you have a role in which you interact with others, etc.

But I've also made other assumptions, like your organization or company (I use them interchangeably in this book, in case you haven't noticed) has values, a mission, a purpose, stated and visible goals, and SOPs. If your organization does not currently have these things, there's an opportunity for you right now to introduce that. These things help define who you are, what you care about, how you think about your work and the way that you think about customers. If you leave these things up to chance, chances are you'll wish you didn't.

Now, in my humble opinion, SOPs can play a crucial role in building this foundation, because these are not just words on a page. They're a reminder for you and everyone on your team on what it takes to operate smoothly and effectively while prioritizing everyone's well-being.

But let's go a bit deeper.

What Are Standard Operating Procedures (SOPs)?

SOPs are detailed, written instructions designed to achieve uniformity in the performance of specific functions. They serve as a roadmap for employees, outlining the best practices and processes required to complete tasks consistently and efficiently. These are usually the results of learnings done over time, similarly to FAQs, but not public or consumer-facing.

The Importance of SOPs in an Organization

Why do we need SOPs? We don't, but the purpose of this book is to help you operationalize the empathetic frameworks to achieve maximum results. SOPs help you do that by providing:

- Consistency: SOPs ensure that tasks are performed the same way every time, reducing variability and maintaining high standards.
- Efficiency: Clear instructions streamline processes, saving time and resources.
- Training and Onboarding: SOPs provide new employees with a comprehensive guide, making the onboarding process smoother and faster.

- Quality Control: By following standardized procedures, organizations can maintain a high level of quality in their products and services.
- Compliance and Safety: SOPs help ensure that all legal and safety requirements are met, protecting both the organization and its employees.

Designing SOPs with Empathy in Mind

Creating SOPs is not only about efficiency; it's also about considering the needs and well-being of your team. "Empathetic" SOPs are user-friendly, supportive, and designed to empower employees.

So, how do you create them?

If you've ever worked in an overly friendly or sometimes toxic 'work is family' type of environment, you've seen employees involved in every aspect of every decision. This is usually due to gross misunderstanding of leadership at the top of an organization.

Leadership is neither decision-making in a vacuum or decision making by committee. Its certainty based on experience, leverage, confidence, and a little bit of luck. And it's the fearlessness and ability to pivot when the data or circumstances change.

Here are some guiding principles on how to effectively design SOPs that improve your teams and help them have autonomy in their work:

- Involve Employees: Include team members in the creation of SOPs to ensure that their insights and experiences are reflected. This should be a quarterly or at least, bi-annually reviewed, living document. Things change, people change, processes improve. This will help to create a sense of ownership and ensures the procedures are practical and realistic.

- Clarity and Simplicity: Write SOPs in clear, straightforward language. Avoid jargon and overly complex BS fluff. When necessary or helpful, use visuals like flowcharts and diagrams if they will help with processing the information.
- Flexibility and Adaptability: Allow room for flexibility. All situations are not the same and employees may need to adapt procedures to specific circumstances.
- Continuous Improvement: Encourage feedback and regularly update SOPs based on employee experiences and suggestions.
- Group Authorship: Each employee should feel a sense of ownership over your team's SOPs. If you're the only one who can write them, but you never know what the team is dealing with… Well, you already know what I'm going to say... Leading top down is NOT an optimum way to build a team culture.

Implementing SOPs Effectively

The implementation of SOPs is as important as their creation. Proper rollout strategies can prevent employees from misunderstanding and or failing to adopt the new procedures seamlessly.

Remember this when launching your SOP process:

- Communicate Clearly: Clearly communicate the purpose and benefits of the new SOPs to all employees. Explain how they will improve work processes and contribute to a better work environment.
- Training and Support: Provide comprehensive training sessions to ensure that all employees understand the new procedures. Offer ongoing support and resources to help them adapt.
- Lead by Example: Ensure that leaders and managers model the behaviors outlined in the SOPs. This sets a positive example and reinforces the importance of the procedures.

- Gradual Implementation: Roll out new SOPs gradually to allow employees time to adjust. Start with a pilot phase to gather initial feedback and make necessary adjustments before full implementation.

If you're starting to make the connection, there's a deliberateness and intentionality around leveraging empathy as a part of your toolkit. It is not something you can "wing." When I said earlier people can tell, this is what I meant. Your processes will suck, and the rollout will fall flat.

Methods for Regularly Reviewing and Updating SOPs

As I mentioned, your SOPs will need to be updated, and whether you choose once a year or more frequently, they should be included in any regular team checkups.

Once again, let's review the things you can do to make SOP review a part of your process:

- Scheduling: Set regular intervals (e.g., quarterly or annually) for reviewing and updating SOPs. This ensures they remain current and effective.
- Feedback Loops: Create channels for employees to provide feedback on SOPs. This could be through surveys or regular team meetings.
- Metrics: Use metrics to assess the effectiveness of SOPs. Identify areas where procedures may be falling short and make necessary improvements.
- Employee Involvement: Involve employees in the review process to gather diverse perspectives and insights. This can lead to more practical and effective updates.

SOPs are more than just a set of rules; they are essential tools that guide your team towards success while prioritizing their well-being. When you design SOPs with empathy, implement them effectively, and continuously improve them based on employee feedback, you create a work environment where everyone can excel.

We are building a system for allowing people to feel valued and supported, so they not only perform better, but also feel responsible for building a workplace culture they are proud of.

Chapter 3: Retaining an Empathetic Team

Building an empathetic team is where we begin; retaining that team is where the real challenge lies.

In this chapter, we will discuss the critical role empathy plays in employee retention and provide actionable strategies to keep your team satisfied, committed, and fired up.

The Role of Empathy in Team Retention

You should think of empathy as the catalyst for satisfaction and loyalty. When you feel seen, recognized and respected, isn't it easier for someone to keep your attention? Isn't it easier to defuse a problem situation?

That's the point.

Empathy is more than a soft skill; it is a cornerstone of employee satisfaction and loyalty. When leaders show genuine concern for their team's well-being, it fosters a culture of trust and respect. It makes everything else easier.

It is for this reason that employees who feel valued and understood are more likely to stay with an organization, contribute their best work, and advocate for that company.

People are always going to talk, especially at work, so at least decide what you would like them to say!

The Cost of High Turnover and the Benefits of Retention

High employee turnover is costly—financially and culturally. Recruiting, hiring, and training new employees requires significant time and resources. Frequent turnover can disrupt team dynamics, lower the morale, and reduce overall productivity.

Think about this: it is better to acquire and then keep your customers. Employee retention works the same way.

It also has a much better impact, since retaining employees leads to:

- Increased Productivity: Experienced employees are more efficient and effective in their roles.
- Enhanced Morale: Stable teams foster stronger relationships and a more positive work environment.
- Cost Savings: Reduced recruitment and training expenses free up resources for other initiatives.
- Knowledge Retention: Long-term employees hold valuable institutional knowledge that can drive innovation and improvement.

Building a Supportive Work Environment

You now know that creating a supportive work environment is essential for inviting your team to be more empathetic. But how do you make sure such an environment is possible?

Here are some thoughts on how to create a supportive work environment, and help employees do the same.

- Encourage Open Communication: Create channels for employees to share their thoughts, concerns, and feedback without fear of judgment or retaliation.
- Recognize and Reward Empathy: Acknowledge acts of kindness, support, and empathy within the team. As we discussed previously, your job is to model the behavior, but it's also to incentivize these values as people begin to shift towards more empathetic behavior.
- Promote Work-Life Balance: Encourage employees to take breaks, use their vacation

days, and maintain a healthy work-life balance. If they're always with you, and they hate you, guess how much they're going to love work?
- Foster Inclusion and Belonging: Create an inclusive environment where all employees feel valued and respected, regardless of their background or role.

Remember, you must set the tone because you're trying to shift the culture. All leaders play a crucial role in shaping the workplace culture, but not everyone knows they're a leader. Not everyone is invited to lead.

When you model empathetic behavior, by being understanding, and meeting people where they are, whether they win or lose you're setting the tone for the entire organization.

From this day forward, you can never say you didn't know how to be empathetic. Your responsibilities will now require:

- Leading by Example: Demonstrate empathy in your interactions with employees, showing that you value and respect their experiences and knowledge.
- Providing Training and Development: Don't horde your experience, access, or resources. Make sure to share your ideas freely, and don't do anything you—yourself—would not do. Try to offer training programs that focus on developing (empathetic) leadership skills, in addition to functional job trainings.
- Being Approachable: Make yourself accessible to employees, showing that you are available to listen and support them. Coaching is an all year round job--You don't only coach during the season.

Strategies for Empathetic Leadership

Empathetic leadership is about more than understanding others; it's about taking action to support and uplift the people around you. You must do what you say and say what you do.

Here are some necessary traits you must develop to lead with empathy:

- Active Listening: Practice active listening by giving your full attention to the speaker, acknowledging their feelings, and responding thoughtfully. When possible, try not to multitask and schedule your time outside of meetings for responding to emails and texts.
- Compassionate Communication: Use compassionate language that shows understanding and respect. Avoid dismissive or critical remarks. This is not about punching down.
- Personal Check-Ins: Regularly check in with team members on a personal level, showing genuine interest in their well-being. This doesn't mean you have to cross boundaries, but it does help if you know that the reason the person is working for you is because they've got a kid on the way.
- Transparent Decision-Making: Be transparent about decisions that affect the

team, explaining the reasoning and considering their input. While you may not always be able to let them in on what is happening above their heads, you can make sure they're aware of any changes to their work and roles.
- Be Supportive: Offer support and resources during difficult times, whether it's a work-related challenge or a personal issue. Again, within reason, and with appropriate boundaries.

There may be a part of you that is concerned about this. Perhaps the culture is not one where you feel as though it would be accepted, or well received for someone in leadership to be more curious or sensitive to their colleagues or team's needs. However, I'd argue that your doubts and fears are what is preventing your team from growing together.

Even small shifts can be important to develop an interest in a colleague in a respective manner, like:

- Maintaining Eye Contact: Show that you are fully engaged in the conversation.
- Asking Open-Ended Questions: Encourage employees to share more about their experiences and feelings.
- Reflect and Validate: Mirror what you hear and validate their emotions and perspective, showing that you understand and respect where they're coming from.

Handling Conflict with Empathy

Conflict is inevitable in the workplace, but it doesn't have to be destructive. In my other ebook, "The Empathy Revolution" I share that there are some examples of good and bad conflict. For starters, handling conflict with empathy can help keep bad situations from becoming worse.

Some of the most common workplace conflicts have a suitable, and easy to deploy empathetic response. For every miscommunication, you can repeat back what you heard and ask if that was intended. This encourages clear and open communication to prevent misunderstandings. In every different perspective, is a chance to navigate the complexity of diversity, and that it's not race or religion or gender or orientation that puts us at odds, but our viewpoints. When viewpoints and experiences are not respected and considered, people feel slighted. For every person who has ever felt like they had more work, there was someone who wasn't given a shot to prove themselves at something new. Individual capacity management and redistributing tasks fairly do not require empathy, just clarity.

All conflict requires a steady hand to navigate. I spent a lot of time thinking about the good and bad conflicts, the types that bring teams further together because they trust each other and want to problem solve, versus the type that make people want to rip each other's throats out.

In each case, there are useful steps that anyone can take to defuse the situation:

- Acknowledge the Conflict: Recognize and acknowledge the existence of the conflict without assigning blame.
- Understand All Perspectives: Listen to all parties involved, seeking to understand their viewpoints and feelings.
- Identify Common Goals: Focus on shared goals and interests to find common ground.
- Develop Collaborative Solutions: Work together to develop solutions that address everyone's concerns and needs.
- Follow Up: Monitor the situation and follow up to ensure the resolution is effective and lasting.

I could lie to you and tell you that empathy makes everything better, and people will never be at each other's throats. But that's not true.

You want A+ players because they do have a bit of a chip on their shoulder. You want them to have a little ego and pride in their work. They want to win. But they don't have to knock down anyone else to do it. And neither do you.

Empathy requires you to lead and grow *with* your people. Retaining an empathetic team is not just about reducing turnover; it's about creating a thriving, high-performing workplace.

When you build a supportive environment, lead with empathy, and handle conflicts compassionately, you can cultivate a loyal and engaged team that drives success.
As we continue through the book, you'll continue to learn about the power of empathy in leadership. The true strength of any company lies in its people—and when people feel like belong, they become the prize.

Chapter 4: Positive Relationships

I know, I know. Work is hard. If it was fun, it'd be play.
But don't give up on me now.

Positive relationships in the workplace are essential for an engaged, bustling culture. In this chapter, we will explore how positive relationships can help you do your job, enhance your people's productivity, and make people want to deal with the hard stuff at work.

The Impact of Positive Relationships on Performance

Did you know that there's a link between positive relationships and productivity? Of course you didn't. You've never thought about it before now. But flow state comes from the certainty of the repetition of the visualizations of your success.

Research consistently shows that positive workplace relationships are a key driver of productivity. In fact, some people have stayed at jobs because of their connections to people. It's not money, or the title, or the benefits. It's the people.

When employees feel connected to and cheered on by their colleagues, they are more likely to be motivated and committed to their work. They work for each other, not against. Positive interactions lead to increased job satisfaction, reduced stress, and a stronger sense of belonging—all of which contribute to better teams.

Every employee has a role to play. And the employees that everyone hates are killing the vibe. This is because employee engagement is an emotional commitment an employee has to their organization and its goals.

Not having a pleasant time at work every day plays a role in this engagement. When employees experience kindness, support, joy, and respect from their peers and leaders, they are more likely to go above and beyond in their roles.

Engaged employees are not just more productive; they are also more innovative and proactive, driving the work forward.

Building Trust and Rapport

Trust and rapport are the foundation of healthy relationships. Without trust, teams cannot function effectively. You likely know if your team trusts each other already. But here's where it gets interesting—I talk to a lot of managers who don't trust their teams.

If you get anything from this book, I hope you know why that's a bad place to be in.

Should you be in that boat and want to get off, here are some ways to build trust with your team:

- Be Consistent and Reliable: Be consistent in your actions and follow through on

commitments. Reliability builds trust over time.
- Share Information: Do not withhold because you think you're protecting, or worse, "sparing" your team.
- Believe Them: When they share info with you, believe them until you have a reason not to.
- Let Them Try: Hopefully you didn't hire them because you thought they were you. Since they're not you, let them solve problems and learn how to improve. Your way is not the only way.

A big part of your role in leadership is hiring and retention. Personalities matter, and you need to encourage organic, genuine connections among team members. While it's totally okay if not everyone wants to have a beer, maybe ask them and find out?

Genuine connections go beyond professional interactions; they involve personal understanding. Some of the ways you can do that are by organizing team-building activities and sharing experiences in non-pressure situations.

Quick story because I can't stress how important this is: One morning, we came in to discover the head of our dept. was terminated. And not just terminated, walked out of the building without even a chance to grab her things.

As the manager of our vertical, I knew how uncomfortable it would be for my team to all sit at our desks acting as though that did not happen. I quickly fired off an email to our "new" boss, saying that I was taking the team out for some developmental and team-building activities that day. We had lunch together and while we worked together throughout the time, I let them express themselves freely to blow off some steam. The trust was there. We had collectively survived that moment together, and they weren't sulking at their desks pretending nothing was wrong. We could have been victims to our culture, but we met the moment and got closer as a result. The right thing is the right thing.

Collaboration and teamwork matter, but you must know how they work together. When encouraging problem solving, make sure everyone understands the team's goals and their individual roles in achieving them. When teams are strong, you rarely have to say what everyone's role is to them, because everyone plays their part.

A lot of people like tools and platforms that facilitate collaboration, but your project management software and apps are only as good as the people behind the keyboards.

Look at your team meetings. Are you discussing progress, sharing ideas, and addressing challenges? Are you sharing wins? Are people genuinely excited for one another? There's your focus group for the importance of shared goals, team spirit, and the greater good. Start using it wisely.
Shared goals unify the team and provide a North Star. When they lift each other up, it strengthens

their connection to one another. No one feels isolated or overwhelmed, leading to a more resilient team. This is what we want.

Maintaining Positive Relationships Over Time

You can't set it and forget it. Are you sensing the theme yet? You must keep doing this stuff. Nurturing relationships requires ongoing effort and attention. Think of it like sales. You need a warm prospect to convert. Same thing here.

Which brings me to why retention of teams matters so much. Because you don't want to make your life, and the people's lives who stay, harder. When the team changes it disrupts established relationships, and when workloads start to get unwieldy, it will strain relationships and reduce the capacity and desire to connect.

Transitions happen, it is inevitable. But now that you know what to do to keep your team together, and make that time maybe more positive than negative, I fully expect to be invited to the next team offsite.

The importance of your relationships cannot be overstated. When you build trust, encourage genuine connections and collaboration, you'll create a team dynamic that's hard to beat. To maintain these relationships over time, you'll need to get outside of your comfort zone and challenge yourself.

Comfort is nice, but nothing grows there.

Chapter 5: Achieving High Performance through Empathy

We have spent a bit of time together, so I hope you're more convinced by the powers of empathy and how emotional intelligence can be a vital tool to motivate and galvanize your people to achieve results.

Because empathy isn't just a nice-to-have quality. It's *the* quality.

When we create a culture where empathy is the nucleus—not money, not skill, not ego—people find their fifth and sixth gears.

This chapter will explore the profound impact of empathy on performance, and how you can implement empathetic practices.

Now, let's talk about the link between empathy and performance…

How Empathy Drives Performance

Empathy is a superpower that allows leaders and people managers like you to connect on a deeper level, understanding someone's motivations, strengths, fears, wants, and needs. Why do we want that? Because that connection enables us to problem solve at the individual level, and we can achieve a multiplier effect as we empower our people to do the same thing for each other.

These connections are not for show. We are pouring empathy (fuel) into the heart (gas tank) of your organization. This is a repeated effort, a repeated investment into your culture to create the environment necessary for people to focus on what they're good at, without fear of failure, abuse, or toxicity.

We talked about how empathy enhances communication within teams, because people will feel encouraged to share and make productive decisions. When leaders and team members communicate empathetically, they work

TOGETHER. This leads to more efficient problem-solving and creates room for experimentation, as diverse approaches become commonplace.

There are loads of data that shows the positive impact of empathy on workplace performance.

Research by the Center for Creative Leadership found that empathetic leaders are viewed as better performers by their bosses. Another study by Development Dimensions International revealed that empathy is a key driver of employee engagement and retention.

Companies like Google and Salesforce are known for being transformative, inspirational, global behemoths. What most people don't know is that they're both champions of empathetic leadership, and while no workplace is perfect, they consistently rank high in employee satisfaction and performance metrics. Their success displays that empathy is not only compatible with transformation and accountability, but a complement to it.

For the purposes of this book, I explicitly focused on actions to help you treat people like people at work. People on X will tell you that the only way you will succeed is by suffering, then stepping on everyone, and leaving a trail of bodies in your wake as your scratch and crawl your way to the altar of profit, power, and infamy.

I think that's all garbage. You can be competitive, have a bit of a chip on your shoulder, want to win, and still give a crap about people. And when you win? That's the real prize, because you did it the right way.

Ambition drives growth and success. But achievement should never come at the expense of employees. Empathetic leaders find every way to motivate their teams without crushing them.

You find the balance by regulating workloads, managing priorities and expectations, communicating effectively, and encouraging people to do the things they need to do to succeed inside and outside of the office.

Measuring Success with Empathy

Traditional performance metrics usually focus on outcomes, like sales or revenue generated. And money is important, right? It's a signal your experience and contributions are valued. But a more empathetic approach could work in parallel. You could track those KPI, while also incorporating the more human aspects of performance, or Empathetic Performance Indicators (EPI).

How collaborative are they?
How much do they engage with others?
Do they lift others up or tear them down?
Are they generous with their time, skills, knowledge and strategies?

To reinforce an empathetic culture, it's important to acknowledge and reward behaviors that exemplify empathy. We know that recognition and rewards are powerful motivators. These additional metrics can give you a broad view of someone's impact and contributions to the team. This helps with incentives, like promotions, bonuses, salary increases, title changes and other symbols of success at the workplace.

Examining Empathetic Teams

There are many examples of workplaces that achieve success by putting people, not profit, first.

Patagonia's commitment to employee well-being and environmental responsibility has created brand affinity and positive market sentiment, as well as a deeply loyal and high-performing workforce. Their open communication channels, flexible work arrangements, and focus on personal growth have resulted in not only high employee satisfaction, but also explosive growth.

Another example is Microsoft under the leadership of Satya Nadella. Nadella's emphasis on having a growth mindset vs. a fixed mindset, has transformed the company's culture, leading to increases in modernization. By prioritizing empathy, Microsoft has built stronger teams and developed products that exceed customer needs and continue to change as the customer's life changes.

Empathy is truly a force of nature. And while a small percentage of people are "born empaths" many people can practice and become more empathetic. Think of empathy like a muscle.

The more exposure to different cultures, people, and lives you encounter and truly immerse yourself in, the better informed and more inclusive you can be. As you continue to flex the muscle of empathy, you can also become the model of empathy for others.

It's okay if you don't "get it" right away. I am certainly an empathetic practitioner, and one of those natural born empaths. But even I find myself straying from my playbook when I experience disappointment, incompetence, poor communication, lack of engagement or other silly distractions. Ground yourself in the fact that people are mostly trying their best, when they try at all, and we can't see or know what someone else is going through unless we connect with them directly.

Conclusion

As we come to the end of this book, I want to reflect on the insights and strategies we've explored together. In each chapter, the goal was for you to understand how an empathetic framework could help your team and how you could implement it in your own way. In some cases, I could give you some direct strategies to engage your teams more empathetically and to help shape the culture you want.

Let's quickly recap the things we worked on together.

- Chapter 1: The Power of Empathetic Hiring
    - Understanding Empathetic Hiring: Empathetic hiring goes beyond skills and experience, focusing on candidates' emotional intelligence and ability to connect with others.
    - Examples of Empathetic Behaviors to Look For: What are the social cues to

look out for when sourcing candidates for empathy?
- Conducting Empathy-Focused Interviews: Structuring interviews that prioritize empathy foster a more inclusive and supportive hiring process.
- Examples of Successful Empathetic Frameworks in Modern Day Companies: Real-world examples demonstrate the impact of empathetic hiring on team dynamics and performance.
- The Human Potential of People: Unlearn what you think of when thinking of people: profits, expenses, problems, and shift into growing the best and most highly functioning groups of people.
- Looking Ahead: A preview of what is in the rest of the book.

- Chapter 2: Thoughtful SOPs for a Thriving Team
    - What Are Standard Operating Procedures (SOPs)?: SOPs ensure consistency and efficiency, providing a foundation for a well-organized workplace.
    - The Importance of SOPs in an Organization: SOPs consider employee well-being and should be user-friendly and supportive.
    - Implementing SOPs Effectively: Successful implementation requires comprehensive training and ongoing support.
    - Methods for Regularly Reviewing and Updating SOPs: Regular reviews and employee feedback are crucial for maintaining and enhancing SOPs.

- Chapter 3: Retaining an Empathetic Team
    - The Role of Empathy in Team Retention: Empathy significantly contributes to employee satisfaction and loyalty, reducing turnover.
    - The Cost of High Turnover and the Benefits of Retention: Supportive environments foster empathy and strengthens team cohesion, but be warned, it takes work and constant effort.
    - Building a Supportive Work Environment: Practical advice for leading with empathy, including active listening and compassionate communication.
    - Strategies for Empathetic Leadership: Some ideas on how to cultivate an empathetic culture.
    - Handling Conflict with Empathy: Empathetic conflict resolution methods lead to more harmonious and productive workplaces.

- Chapter 4: Positive Relationships
    - The Impact of Positive Relationships on Performance: Positive relationships enhance productivity and employee engagement.
    - Building Trust and Rapport: Strategies for fostering trust and genuine connections within teams.
    - Maintaining Positive Relationships Over Time: Solutions for sustaining strong and productive relationships in the long term.

- Chapter 5: Achieving High Performance through Empathy
    - The Link Between Empathy and Performance: Empathy drives high performance by enhancing communication, engagement, and creativity.
    - How Empathy Drives Performance: Methods for setting ambitious, yet empathetic, goals that consider the people impacted.

- Measuring Success with Empathy: Metrics and rewards that recognize and reinforce empathetic behaviors.
- Examining Empathetic Teams: Examples of successful teams that thrive through empathy-driven practices.

The Future of Leadership is Empathetic

The landscape of leadership is evolving, and empathy is at the forefront of this transformation. Emerging trends in empathetic leadership include the growing emphasis on mental health, the integration of flexible work arrangements, and the use of technology to enhance human connections. As we move forward, the potential impact of empathetic leadership on future workplaces is immense. Companies that embrace empathy will not only attract and retain top talent but also foster innovation and resilience in the face of challenges.

Final Thoughts

You did it.

Thanks for reading "The People Are the Prize," my love letter to teams.

I hope you come away with a resolve to make your workplaces more functional, less toxic, and more productive. You should be nervous and excited, and maybe a little unsure on where you go from here. But you don't need to be Microsoft or Patagonia to create a culture that makes people excited to walk into fire with and for you.

As a reminder: The journey to becoming an empathetic leader is within everyone's reach. Remember: Empathy is a muscle.

Embrace the Journey

My own path has been filled with ups and downs, enough to be in a completely and much longer book. It's not easy to lead. So many of us want to be chosen and appointed as the leader.

I came to leadership through a sweeping, muddy road that was never clear to me at the time. You put it all on the line, every time. I've been an intern, an advisor, and worked at or with some of the world's biggest companies. Here's what I know: Whether it's in a boardroom or a coffee shop, leadership rooted in empathy works. You don't need anyone's permission.

Empathy connects us.

Your journey will have its own unique ups and downs. Embrace them. Use every experience to refine your approach and strengthen your commitment. If you encounter pushbacks to your shift towards a more empathetic, compassionate workplace, keep going. Know that each step you take towards empathetic leadership is a step towards a more inclusive and dynamic workplace.

Motivated Empowerment

You should feel as though you have some tools and insights that you can use in your meetings, in your performance reviews, and in your team building activities going forward. You have the potential to make a profound impact. Start small if you need to—initiate one empathetic practice, refine one SOP, have one meaningful conversation. These small actions will accumulate, creating a culture where empathy is the norm, not the exception. Small things equal big things.

Remember, you are not alone in this. You're now officially in the club. I am happy to welcome you to this beautiful and expansive community who are committed to making empathy the cornerstone of their leadership style.

Let's all commit to create workplaces where everyone feels valued, heard, and motivated to give their best.

The People Are the Prize

Never forget that your team members are your most valuable assets.

They are not just employees; they are the heartbeat of your organization. Investing in their growth, well-being, and happiness will yield the greatest returns.

Our job as leaders is not just to guide and direct, but to grow alongside our people. We also must evolve. Too often, we forget that our development is as crucial as theirs.

I have a sense of deep gratitude and boundless optimism for the work you will do to empower others. Your commitment to this process, is not just a commitment to doing better business; it's a commitment to making a better world.

Stay aware, stay open, and continue to lead fearlessly.

The future of leadership is empathetic, and the people are the prize, not the profit.

Index

A

- Active Listening
- Analysis of Impact on Teams and Performance

B

- Balancing Ambitious Targets with Empathy
- Benefits of Empathetic Hiring
- Building Trust and Rapport
- Building a Supportive Work Environment

C

- Case Studies of High-Performance Empathetic Teams
- Common Workplace Conflicts and Empathetic Approaches
- Conducting Empathy-Focused Interviews
- Conflict Resolution Framework Based on Empathy

- Contribution of SOPs to Consistency and Efficiency

D

- Definition and Concept of Empathetic Hiring
- Designing SOPs with Empathy in Mind

E

- Empathy and Performance
- Empathy in Leadership
- Emerging Trends in Empathetic Leadership
- Encouraging Collaboration and Teamwork
- Examples of Empathetic Behaviors
- Examples of Teams Achieving Success through Empathy

F

- Final Thoughts

G

- Guidelines for Creating Empathetic SOPs

H

- Handling Conflict with Empathy
- How Empathy Contributes to Employee Satisfaction and Loyalty
- How Empathy Drives High Performance

I

- Identifying Empathy in Candidates
- Importance of Shared Goals and Mutual Support
- Importance of Training and Support
- Implementing SOPs Effectively
- Impact of Positive Relationships on Performance
- Introduction

K

- Key Questions to Ask in Interviews

L

- Leadership in Setting the Tone
- Leveraging Positive Relationships

- Looking Ahead

M

- Maintaining Positive Relationships Over Time
- Measuring Success with Empathy
- Methods for Regularly Reviewing and Updating SOPs
- Monitoring and Improving SOPs
- Motivated Empowerment

O

- Overview of the Book

P

- Practical Advice for Leading with Empathy

R

- Recap of Key Points
- Real-World Examples of Empathetic Hiring
- Recognizing and Rewarding Empathetic Behaviors

- Research on Positive Relationships and Productivity
- Retaining an Empathetic Team
- Role of Empathy in Team Retention
- Role of Leadership in Setting the Tone

S

- Setting Empathetic Goals
- Standard Operating Procedures (SOPs)
- Strategies for Empathetic Leadership
- Strategies for Rolling Out New SOPs
- Summary of Main Takeaways from Each Chapter
- Techniques for Active Listening and Compassionate Communication
- Techniques for Identifying Empathy in Interviewees
- Techniques for Promoting Collaboration and Teamwork
- The Importance of Empathy in Leadership
- The Link Between Empathy and Performance
- The People Are the Prize

- Tips for Creating a Supportive and Empathetic Work Environment
- Tips for Fostering Genuine Connections Among Team Members
- Tips for Making SOPs User-Friendly and Supportive
- Transforming Workplace Dynamics with Empathy

U

- Understanding Empathetic Hiring
- User-Friendly SOPs

References / Recommended Reading

Bersin, J. (2020). Empathy in Business: Why It Matters and How to Cultivate It. *Harvard Business Review*. Retrieved from https://hbr.org/2020/03/empathy-in-business-why-it-matters-and-how-to-cultivate-it

Brown, B. (2018). *Dare to Lead: Brave Work. Tough Conversations. Whole Hearts.* New York, NY: Random House.

Covey, S. R. (2004). *The 7 Habits of Highly Effective People: Powerful Lessons in Personal Change.* New York, NY: Free Press.

Duhigg, C. (2016). *Smarter Faster Better: The Secrets of Being Productive in Life and Business.* New York, NY: Random House.

Goleman, D. (2006). *Social Intelligence: The New Science of Human Relationships.* New York, NY: Bantam Books.

Grant, A. (2013). *Give and Take: Why Helping Others Drives Our Success*. New York, NY: Viking.

Kouzes, J. M., & Posner, B. Z. (2017). *The Leadership Challenge: How to Make Extraordinary Things Happen in Organizations* (6th ed.). Hoboken, NJ: Wiley.

Lencioni, P. M. (2002). *The Five Dysfunctions of a Team: A Leadership Fable*. San Francisco, CA: Jossey-Bass.

Rath, T., & Conchie, B. (2008). *Strengths Based Leadership: Great Leaders, Teams, and Why People Follow*. New York, NY: Gallup Press.

Rock, D. (2009). *Your Brain at Work: Strategies for Overcoming Distraction, Regaining Focus, and Working Smarter All Day Long*. New York, NY: Harper Business.

Sinek, S. (2009). *Start with Why: How Great Leaders Inspire Everyone to Take Action*. New York, NY: Portfolio.

Thomas, K. W. (2009). *Intrinsic Motivation at Work: What Really Drives Employee Engagement* (2nd ed.). San Francisco, CA: Berrett-Koehler Publishers.

The Empathetic Leader is Kristina Villarini's company for coaching, training, and "empathetic re-programming."

If you're interested in learning more about us, please visit: www.theempatheticleader.com.

THANK YOU.